The Night Divers

Also by Melanie McCabe

POETRY
History of the Body
What the Neighbors Know

NON-FICTION
His Other Life: Searching for My Father,
His First Wife, and Tennessee Williams

The Night Divers

Terrapin Books

Terrapin Books
4 Midvale Avenue
West Caldwell, NJ 07006

www.terrapinbooks.com

ISBN: 978-1-947896-57-4
Library of Congress Control Number: 2022939878

First Edition

Cover art: *The Night Swim*
by Kat O'Connor, 2016
Oil on Wood, 41" X 31"

Cover Design: Diane Lockward

In memory of my sister, Terri

Contents

If Time Travel Is Possible

Physicists concur that if time travel is possible
it will be only in one direction, into a future

filled with people I do not know, towns
so rearranged and remade that I would need

a guide to walk the landscape I once claimed
as mine, the streets that I could tick off and tally

like beads in a well-ordered prayer. Something
about traveling backwards would confound

the past, introduce *now* into *then*, and unravel
the orderly progression of what happened

and what happened next. I am no scientist, but
I've watched *Back to the Future*, and so I know

the risk of my own disappearance, the wrong
strings I might pull that could tangle the marionettes

of my history. But Marty McFly's mistake
was opening his mouth—being seen. That is why

my own plan is foolproof. I do not want to return
as an actor to the scene, but as a viewer. A voyeur.

A Peeping Me at the window of my childhood,
able to follow my younger self as I move through

the house, to peer into other windows and listen in
on conversations my parents had while I was sleeping.

It would be enough to watch and then to watch
once more the reels of those days spin out, the effect

like the lull and comfort of an old movie returned to,
again and again, because it soothes, because of the calm

that comes from knowing before it even begins
that the end is only the end until you start over.

One

The Night Divers

Each night we dropped quarters for each other
into the shaking green light of the hotel pool,
testing our mettle and our lungs in the still

scary plunge into the deep end. Less than an hour
from closing, we were often the only swimmers
in this abandoned world, all other children

out on the teeming boardwalk, appended
to a parent's hand, or already bathed, pajama'd,
lulled in the laugh track of a sitcom, struggling

to stay awake through a flickering blue hypnosis.
My sister and I were proud rebels in our contrary
allegiance to this chlorine-scented center

of the earth, ringed by balconies draped in bright
beach towels, forsaken by those who chose
to confine their holidays to sunlight and hubbub.

If far-off we could hear the bells and cries
of Funland or the shrieks of teenagers chasing
the selves they were becoming faster than they knew,

that ruckus could be swallowed and expunged
by one dive into the water where bubbles
and our heartbeats were the only sounds that lasted.

I have no memory of being watched, though I suppose
we were. What has stayed with me all these years later
is only our two bodies, pushing, kicking, again and again,

toward a bottom that was lit and well-marked, and then,
the quick pivot, the surge for air that we never doubted
would be awaiting us when we returned for it.

Capitulations

I would still, someday, like to be fathomed, my measure taken
to a sea floor rippling with the luminescent nameless.

Plumbed, I might also long to be combed and delved.
Even at the surface, I have yearned to be stirred and phosphoresced,

cells switched on by passage through of swimmer or craft.
I crave an agitation that my light might be cajoled.

A myth, I might yet be proven true—an Atlantis rising
to rub her belly against Morocco's sleeping spine,

revealed, possessed at last by a flag whipping the air
of the border I forgot to guard.

Incursion

Alerted by the scratching and scrabbling
of claws against metal, the scraping
and scuffling of feathered heft, of pecking,

I hear them first through the walls
when I am two floors below, but cannot name
or pinpoint the source; I only know

this growing uneasiness that something
is amiss, that my closed-door, paid-for silence
has been infiltrated by a foreign presence,

an intruder I sense means me no good.
Outside, looking up, I can just make out
dark shapes moving inside the latticed guards

that let in rain but should prevent breach
by starling or sparrow. What most unsettles me
is that I see but cannot see, that they are a specter

without a name. I know by their telltale shifting,
abrading, that they are real, that they are filling
with twigs and straw and bramble

what had been clear and free, what had been
egress for storms. How long have they worked here
at this penetration, this slow ruin, without

my detection? What other stealth goes on
without my knowledge? Carpenter bees.
Termites. Mold in some dripping corner,

spreading. Dividing cells. Arteries,
hardening. Bones thinning to snap-kindling.
The sudden swoop of the crow that carried off

my sister two winters ago, though I watched
all night. Though I scanned the skies.
Though I petitioned for reinforcements.

In bed before sleep, I can hear them
settling against each other, beaks tucked
in, wings folded, narrow lungs breathing

their portion of my air. I must live
in this house. I must live in two houses.
At least one of them is riddled by birds.

From the Mountain

Do not be anxious about your life,
this frail thing you keep in a box of cotton.
What you shall eat or what you shall drink
is waiting up a sleeve
or in water hocus-pocused into wine.
Nor about your body, what you shall put on,
for it is gift wrap only and men will shake you
to see what's inside.

Look at the birds of the air—envy them
their thoughtless swoop and wingbeat.
They neither sow nor reap
nor cringe at a pinch of too ample thigh—
and yet for them the mud seethes with worms
and seeds twirl on the wind.

Consider the lilies of the field—
how instinct tips them naked
in the midst of twitching bees,
how they lean to the landing
of buzzer to bloom.
They neither toil nor spin,
yet they are as sated as any lovers tangled
in the white sheets of morning.

Do not be anxious then about your life—
do not pop anodynes, toss back chardonnays,
or cover the sharp edges of your brain with pain-proof

corner guards. Do not obsess about tomorrow,
for tomorrow will obsess about itself—
in fact, is already reading self-help books.
Instead, let the day's own nail-gnaws
be sufficient for the day.
Save your strength for the long nights spent
tallying sheep, for accruing dreams
that would make even Freud afraid.

Tell the Birds

Someone tell the birds we are a world
divided—a spirit, broken. Their calls
over the crosshatch of limbs and green,
over the suddenly opened sky, are pure
and misguided, full of a sound startlingly

like joy. Something primitive, unbidden
in me also rises to see the sun again
after fifteen days of gray and rain—
the ground bogged, the azaleas, brown
and beaten—but it is in my bones only,

and not my brain. I know what I know.
Time cannot flow backwards.
There is a wellspring of something
wholly unholy that pushes toward us
from a dark beneath the breathed and seen.

It was always there. While I wasn't looking—
my eyes instead upward, petitioning the stars.
And while my only sister was busy
with the brutal task of dying
across three long winters—cold snaps

that claimed the faith I had in summer,
in the earth's return. The weight
of those weeks of storm and gloom was truer
than this charlatan sun. Every sham song should be
silenced now. But no one has told the birds.

The Last Time I Was Here, You Were Alive

Every landmark seems changed now, blank,
mere architecture or postcard scene,
holding fast to its secret story, meaning
nothing to the people passing, to the man
who walks beside me, unless I tell it.

That white bench, with its back that flips
to face either sea or carnival games,
is where we sat, untethered from our parents,
to eye the boys let loose after dark—their faces
sunburned; their pedigrees, uncertain.

That balcony, two floors up, third from the left,
is where you watched me leave you behind
in your childhood, while I crossed over
into something more dangerous, beside
the green-lit pool, the scent of chlorine

and coconut oil swaying my judgment,
changing me in your eyes from sister
before to sister after. From every railing,
terry cloth colors blew and spangled, waiting
for morning, while you waited

for me. We passed through decades.
Each summer, returning, we were altered,
appended to different hands, but the ocean

never changed, its repetition a lull,
a gray tale told over and over until

it did the work of prayer. Of litany.
This late June evening, by headlights
and memory, I drive down Surf Avenue, veer
left at Ocean Drive, past the beach club,
searching for that one street on North Shores;

you remember the one, if you can still remember
anything at all. In the dark, I miss it, must
turn around at the state park, return until the name,
Holly Road, sparks a synapse in a long-folded
map, opens up at the history of who you were,

of the woman you tried so hard to find.
That house you rented on a pilgrimage,
intending to stay a month, listening only
for the voice that would declare itself
yours, was filled instead with silence,

and what could you fill that silence with
but fear? That you fled, that you left
the house to me, was a gift
already broken: Here is this hobbled
idyll by the tides; see what you can

make of it. You came here to turn a key
in a lock, to find the solution that would
transform your fraction to a whole.

You didn't know then that this quest would be
the work of your life, or that your life

would end so soon. Tonight the house
is as empty as it was forty years ago.
I am quiet all the long drive back,
window down so I can listen to the sea
repeating what it thought I already knew.

Home Movies

These dusty 8-millimeter reels
resurrect my father. We roll back the stone,
project him alive to a tacked-up
white sheet, his face concave in a wrinkle.

At the mercy of that handheld jitter,
he ricochets from shadow to glare,
so that I have to squint hard to see
that this ghost wears bones I know.

White-hot, the projector's light
dances with dust-mote angels. Silence,
it seems, can also carry messages
when the ear surrenders sound.

Our younger selves wave
at a future we can't yet imagine.
Across the front lawn, my father executes
a perfect cartwheel. More than

anything else on this reel, that
cartwheel summons for me
who he was and how he lived his life.
Before me, played out in mime,

we stare into the camera's eye,
lips testifying to forgotten stories.
Two sisters unscroll an ancient script
and call into an empty tomb.

Language Lessons

I am being schooled in the tongue that is spoken here:
the white crackle, the hiss that hoards the air
of my small glass life. Words I might have said

buzz in the air, unglossed, and tick against
the windows like moths. Static, that long
knell, becomes the sound I take for silence.

My syllables coalesce to drone, to hum—still, I
think first in the old language—the wind-rippled
chime, the patois of leaves at the eaves of the house.

When all of my desire flattens to a chord held long
beneath a damper pedal, I will at last be eloquent
in the idiom of this changed world. But for now I still know

sparrows in the limbs outside, turning gingerly to spare
their straw bones. I dream with them of other
mornings, of lifting high a brave and foolish throat.

Endangered

Save us before we disappear behind gleaming screens,
before we no longer find tongues to carry our frantic words.

Save us while we tremble at the anthers of late blooms
for a ration of nectar in our parched mouths.

Act now. Breathe back into our tightening throats
the coin and jingle of oxygen, the lulling anaphora

of the said-before, the call and refrain of the lungs
to the air. Pledge to hold us inside our skins,

inside our jackstraw and tenuous bones. Call
back the buzz, the exodus from the gassed hive.

Seal broken shells; fill them with hubbub and wings.
Sign new rings into the trunk of the narrow tree.

Guard us like condor, ocelot, and tamarin.
Guard us like mink and ivory and whale song.

Help us move through the darkness with our failing eyes.
Light up the dormant switchboard with stars.

Two

Estranged

The ocean turns over without me there to see it, hurls its churn
and froth, its broken shells up against the sand I have traveled
so far away from to arrive in this landlocked place. I am
not doubtful about the sea.

                It will be where I left it when I return.

The gulls will go on, as well—one a twin to the next, dragging across
the sky the same disgruntled squawking of the year before
and the year before that. Beyond the wave break,
the gray arcs of dolphins

                will repeat themselves.

Perhaps then, you, too, continue. I like to imagine your silhouette
at the end of one of those private docks on Silver Lake, the ones
we knew we mustn't trespass on—your feet dangling over
the moving water as the sun plays over

                mysteries you cannot yet tell me.

I remember our days, fanned before me like a deck of cards.
If you could say to me now, *Pick a day, any day*, no matter
which I chose, it would be the right one. There was no day then
that ended without you;

                no moment had arrived that foretold this one.

Ocean

Ocean to me is close enough to God—gray,
impenetrable, tide-muscled, a brawler. Unseen
fist that has clouted me airless more than once.

Repetitive. Answer always oblique, spitting
its sharps in harangues of salt, its froth in murmur.
Abrader and buoy, both. Antagonist. Beguiler.

A cradle, but also, the scene of the crime; I return
and return. Not braving pummel, but submitting
to it. At smack of wave, offering only the body's

negotiations. Over me, a choir of gulls, their one
note, indignant. Each inch forward, a reluctant
confession. Each inch backward, a pardon in sand.

If There Are Ghosts

If there are ghosts, they are hapless. Not even
crafty enough to rap upon the glass or help the wind
to push open a door we thought was closed. Somewhere

they must rail at their inefficacy, must kick
in pique at the impotence of their changed selves. If
they have voices, not even dogs can hear them.

If ghosts have a language we can listen to, then it is
static. White noise. Something so omnipresent
that we have to remind ourselves it is always

there in the air just below the air we know.
If we invite them in, bid them sit down in the chair
we've drawn up next to our own, how will we know

if they have complied? Not even the heat
of our palms that we extend in supplication
will alter a degree, though perhaps their own hands

answered ours as soon as we asked, covered ours
with a colorless and glacial longing. They are poor
advertisements for the other side. We pine

for testimonials, a four-star system of reviews, before
committing ourselves. But the dead are lousy salesmen.
And we must purchase, nonetheless.

Status Update

I sometimes fantasize that there could be a one-stop
cosmetic-surgery fix-it shop—something like a carwash,
where I'd pay my crisp green bills into a machine, then
hit the button marked "as needed" and tracks beneath
the wheels would begin to tug me through a total,
premium bells-and-whistles upgrade—and inside,
while I leaned back, humming, I could watch
amazing scrubbing tightening paring erasing
bubbles cascade over me, while
sponges clippers sanders polishers moved at whip-fast,
pain-free speed, and all I'd hear would be a lulling
whoosh or maybe 8-track tapes playing tunes
I used to be beautiful to, and when at last I lurched
off the conveyor into the sunshine, I'd be tucked, taut,
unpocked, unmarred, lush, lithe and zipping with lust, but
smarter somehow than I ever was when I looked
like this before, and moreover, now my car would be
a Jaguar. Red. Dazzling. Its motor, gunned.

The Sound of It

Every August night knew the hum of that old Deco fan
my father brought to the marriage from his apartment
in the city. I threw my voice into its dangerous
blades to hear myself warble as if underwater.

A darker song pressed itself against the screens,
mingled with crickets, with the turning over
of Chevy engines, their sudden radios blaring Motown
or the Stones. It was there in the laughter that broke

the night, in the shrieks of teenagers I'd been told
were up to no good, or in the blue streak cussed
by the man with open windows and a wife none of us
had ever heard. I felt that song in the floorboards,

in the pounded ground where my sister ran and trapped
lightning in her tight hands. But from the kitchen,
my mother sang hymns above a percussion of plates
and silver settling back into drawers. That clink of knife

on knife, spoon on spoon, just beneath her gospel,
beneath that burden she would lay by the riverside,
became for me a bass line—a rhythm I let lull me into living
as though someone waited for me on that far shore.

Flock Call

The air denies winter, so warm I unzip
my coat, contemplate shedding it—
and might, if not for the burden and bulk
it would make in my arms. What stops
my pace is birdsong from a thicket
of bare and tangled branches—

but not really song. Cacophony.
A choir of shrill. So many throats
repeating the same note that it seems
the brambled whole is speaking
to me. Such a crosshatch of limbs
and rustlings, I cannot see

the birds at first, then only a lifted wing
that tells me: sparrows. My walk
has just begun, so I move on, but plan
to circle back, somehow needing to know
if they will still be at it, to learn how long
this wind that does not constrict,

but rather, opens the body back into
light, can impel such a chittering
mayhem of sound. In the eastern sky,
the smudge of a half-moon hangs
as a kind of confession to those
who know to look for signs,

who have seen the long-range forecast
of a bitter snap, highs only in the teens
just days away, who know the shill at work
in this breeze that frees the damp scent
of waking earth into a world
that should be locked in ice.

On my return, I pass by a forsythia
duped into bloom, its sticks tricked into
surrendering their yellow buds too soon.
The flowers wave dumbly on passing
gusts of diesel fumes and engine whine
from the road I walk down.

At length, I come back to the tightly woven
hedge, to what I have named as I walked,
the church of the sparrows. From inside
its crisscrossed rafters, brown shadows
flicker and change, and yet, they are still
singing— devout, beguiled.

Point of View

The end of your rope is not so terrible if
you have a knot to ride on. Out over
the murky green in a circle of breeze
and billow, the instinct is still
this tip of your face to rippling
leaves that tease the hint of sky.

You are happy to confide this tale
that spins you a bold arc across
the abyss. It takes verve to arch
the spine and spill the dangle
of your hair, the trail of fingertips
over the far burble, the broken glass.

This fraying rope is not the one you rode
as a child. The circumference drawn
by that old abandon was not as wide;
each revolution returned you to where
you launched your new body into space.
The braid of the rope was not plaited with snap.

Better, perhaps, to linger there,
where each orbit over the tangled reeds,
the clots of moss in the gloom send sun glints
signaling a message you understand—
lulling in its telling, retelling that story
of a girl who did not let go.

The Body, Broken

The body, broken, is a new thing, cleft and then
seamed—the faulty excised; relics, rewired.

The old neighborhood, but houses hide breathers
of a different cadence. Decrescendo. Doloroso.

It is a mystery—cracked, end-tied—the cover
closed on subplot; all of the machinations

of minor characters left to stew. Yet you hear them,
restless in their stories, words muffled by walls.

You know they are not finished being unhappy—
that they will see things through without you.

Your Vanity

I found the polaroid at the bottom of a box
while I was searching for photos to mount
and display at your funeral.
Light and heat and carelessness had not been kind—
the image was jigsawed through with cracks
that made it seem less a ruin and more
some damaged portrait from a Renaissance attic,
your face divided by branching roots,
your expression a fragment of a moment
that seemed so ancient
I couldn't absorb that it was I who had preserved it.

Behind you was your vanity that backed against
the west wall of the bedroom we shared,
its glass top covered in the implements
of your beautifying.
Holding a magnifying glass over the image,
the history of seventeen-year-old you
rose up for me like a ghost
and so I inventoried the artifacts to keep you
from disappearing.

Sixteen bottles of nail enamel,
of Burgundy Pearl, of Nutty Nutmeg,
(marked with a line after each application
so that I would not pilfer even a little).
An econo-jar of Dippity Do, for the wings
that would not, the flyaways that would.

A yellow pump bottle of Sun-In. A curling iron.
An empty Marlboro hard pack, a lighter,
and a gift of Jovan Woman I gave you at Christmas,
full-bodied and still uncorked.
A mirror with a dial to four possible locales—always set
on Evening Light, for a pink and poreless glow.
Six eyelash curlers with the rubber missing
and a tube of waterproof Maybelline
for the eyelashes that survived.

Neither of us had any faith in our own allure
though we labored at it, stone cutters
in a quarry that only grew deeper and emptier,
painters with a palette of infinite color
and only one canvas.

I kept the photo but did not add it to the display.
Who but me would see beyond its damage,
its brittle flaking, to the magic
that appeared in my hand that day in 1978?
We snapped dozens, hovered over each
as they materialized before us—
but this is the one that survives.
You must not have been ready for me to snap the picture
because your smile here is more laughter than smile—
your eyes not coy, but merry.

I kept the photo for myself alone:
evidence—though it was disintegrating—
of who you were when no one was watching.

Three

What Burned in the Sky

Every afternoon that spring, my sister and I hurried home
to catch the narrow, ninety-minute sliver of sun that fell across

our driveway, scraping the aluminum of the latticed
lounge chairs across the bricks to find the perfect angle to tip

our faces, our winter-white bodies, to the sinking light.
Speed was valued, as was teamwork. In early May we began

with Coppertone, our fingers quick over the easily accessible
calves and thighs, bellies and arms, and then, attending

to one another, over the hardest-to-reach places, and finally,
the impossible circles between the shoulder blades.

By June, we had bronzed enough to transition
to baby oil, and sometimes, for the heady scent of it,

to cocoa butter. It was the spring that Deep Purple climbed
the charts, and though our tiny radio with the bent antenna

picked up dozens of other tunes, "Smoke On the Water"
is the only one that I recall, the only song that plays

in my head when I try to resurrect those yellow hours.
That four-measure riff repeats in tandem with the remembered

drone of planes, the nearer hum of bees through moss and violets.
Forty years later, knowing everything that came afterwards,

it seems the only soundtrack that makes any sense at all.
Our time was running out. But the five o'clock church bells

were the deadline we honored then, and they tolled as our sun
was doused behind the oak, as the driveway surrendered to shadows.

It was the hour to go inside. We were certain there would be
more afternoons. We circled with the earth to hurry them.

Heading Home

Aruba, Corsica, Barbados, Crete,
Bahamas, Puerto Rico—somewhere warm.
It doesn't matter where as long as chill
and frost are not a part of forecasts there.

I want to scent my skin with Coppertone,
drink rum-and-cokes or rum-and-rums till dawn,
on pink-hued sand with smiling dark-eyed men
who say my name in island cadences;

to forget for just a time that life is hard,
that you are dying slowly by degrees.
I want to bury what I cannot change
in water warmer than our blood.

Jamaica, Trinidad—turquoise seas
in brochure worlds where perfect people twine,
where scallops dot the shore symmetrically,
and no one's ever sick. And no one dies.

Virginia Square. Then Ballston. East Falls Church.
You count the stops; the Orange Line takes us home.
February. Drizzling. But still I dream
that islands exist where no one's ever cold.

Storm Watch

This intrepid, teetering house on stilts
you have built above a blackwater
snaky with dread.
I knock wood—softly—that no new storm
whips in to plunge you
in that plaguey swamp,
Pig-brave, you face the huff and puff
that shakes the already shaken.

This house leans creaking in a hard wind.
In tilt and keen, at every window
you hang white lace. Its flutter soothes.
Above the din I call to you
Breathe deep, breathe in;
that wild blow—so tropic, rank—
carries wisps of sweet pea
from another time.

This shanty sways you, sister mine,
in splintery visions of rickety sticks.
Instead, dream days of sun-warmed piers,
piney and sure, beneath your skin.
In the pummel and groan—recall, recall,
the easy slap of wave and wood,
the lives we left,
the lull of before.

A Creed

I believe in twilight's insistence of honeysuckle;
in a late sky that paints its scumble of pale
yellow and periwinkle on a canvas of blue;

in the communion we feel in a dim theater or the sorcery
of a page that conjures sorrow outside of ourselves;
in the spine's shiver in a windstorm of impossible notes.

I believe in the cosmos of a cell; in the electron, the quark
and the vibrating string; in both the black hole that collapses
a star and the bang that propels the non into known.

And in the void: something. And on a white screen: words.
And beyond the period: and. And beyond the period: and.
In the name of the bubble from boiling: the resurrection of steam.

The face of the deep leans over my shoulder into the mirror.
In the twain that peers back at me from solitude:
I believe there is something to believe.

This Dog

This dog has barked all day from a yard I cannot pinpoint.
I do not think he has a collar. I do not think he has a name,
or surely someone would have called it—or cursed it.

I suspect that neither does he have
a body except for muzzle, throat and trembling,
but the reverb of his deep yelp punctuates my air.

This bark is the ping-pong, the thrum-whoosh of
blood between my ears; this bark is the white noise
of my waking up and my lying down.

I have chewed my morning cereal in time to this dog.
This bark has been my backbeat as I haul laundry
down the stairs and up again, as I clink the clean

china and silver from dishwasher to shelves.
This bark has been the bass as I peck these keys.
This woof is what's mine when all else is no longer.

This dog has barked all day and I suppose will bark
all night. I will dream dog dreams if I dream at all.
Sleep is the blank slate and all I can know is canine.

All day this dog, this dog, this dog has dogged me
with yowl and pause of yowl, this bark has been
my bouncing ball to follow and chase into a street

of speeding words: *Look both ways; listen*
both ways; and never ask, though you will long to ask,
if anyone else hears this dog.

When the Crows Come

I will not take the enormous crow
as an omen—though it chose
my deck railing to settle on, though
it flexed its scapulae to lift those blue-black wings,
knowing surely how that plumage would catch
the light—the light I reveled in until
that sheen gleamed and flashed
its message across
the afternoon I dared to enter.

This corvid knows me for what I am—
an intruder in its realm. One of the banished.
Even though I do not move, I stir
the air with my persistent breathing.
The crow tilts back its head to the sun
and opens its throat, releasing
a raucous caw that calls down
from high limbs
a second one and then a third.

Even when I slowly rise,
edging toward the door behind me,
they do not suspend their judgment,
their waiting.
Turning back to watch them,
crosshatched now through the mesh screen,
their scene plays out unbroken.
I know the part that is mine in this tale.
I have seen this film before.

A Title Is Beyond Me

I refrain from asking your advice because I am so sure you will give it.

Busy as you are, bustling, accomplishing, I do not doubt you would make
time for me, would bend to lift my chin from my collarbone and recite
folk wisdom about ants and tortoises, medical edicts on posture.

Anaerobia is not a mythic land. I have settled in the valley of sloth
and am too tired to feel bad about it. My pulse appends like a news feed;
I need only sit and watch it flicker to convince myself I am breathing.

Yesterday I posted a status update, and tomorrow I will post another.
This is what I call industry. The future is always hidden from the passenger
sitting backwards on the train. I am grateful for the seat, if not

the velocity of the ride. I envy you your to-do list struck through
with horizontal slashes, your puritan zeal. Tasks accumulate here
like laundry and so I pass a moment or three remembering the scent

of a clean shirt pulled wind-whipped from a clothesline. I spend
an hour more staring out the window at the way the sunlight divides
into moving shapes through the jigsaw of limbs and wishing

I had the vim to go outside. Unwilling to trust my memory, I calculate
the distance between now and then and discover that I was wrong.
Somewhere I am not, the ocean repeats itself. In some moment that is

no longer, a girl rides a red Schwinn and lets go of the handlebars.
A word teeters at the edge of ennui; I write it down and don't erase it.
I tap out long lines to let you know I recall what it means to persevere.

Martyr

I permit myself neither opiate nor anodyne.

I poke my finger straight into the socket—
press my tongue hard to the ice-slick chain link.

The syllables of your name stud the air I pull
back into my lungs, so that even oxygen hurts.

I tug you on in the first pink of morning
like impractical shoes—chosen

to hobble me with precarious heels, to coax
new blisters before the old can callous.

Mine is a penance you would never have asked for.
But I must atone for living in this world

without you. I count off days like rosary beads.
I scrimp on my ration of sun.

Four

Those Summers

In those days, morning was a million miles from night.
Like soft Bazooka or taffy pulled sweet and long,
we stretched out each day until it seemed infinite.

I played kickball, tag and spud in the tar-hot street,
and lived on Frosted Flakes. Fizzies. Stolen Tang.
No matter the day, morning was miles away from night.

I danced in my pajamas until firefly light
studded the darkness with yellow-green glimmering.
We stretched out each day until it seemed infinite.

No grown-up marred this universe; my lone orbit
was singular and charmed. Nothing would dare go wrong
in those days. Morning was a million miles from night,

milk cartons were free of faces. No vile misfit
skulked playgrounds for new prey; the world was still too young.
We stretched farther each day. Tomorrow, finite

and cramped, had yet to arrive—though we knew it might.
The future was a kite we clutched by a long string.
Back then, morning was still a million miles from night.
Each dawn, a new-made thing; our lives, still infinite.

Returning

Sun, flat as a Necco wafer, traces
an orange chalk line down turquoise
to melt on the tongue of the river.
The breeze rings through the bells
of the boats; the sails ripple and whip.

Belly-down on the boards of our dock,
I press my face into warped planks
to breathe remembered wood and brine,
to let my skin take in heat
the grain retained from noon.

Late afternoon turns on the axis
of an upriver mast.
The sky before black is indigo.
Stars leak through, and behind me,
woods tune.

At the edge, I dangle my feet
into moving dark, swirl them in arcs
to watch the water transmute to glow,
to remember those nights our feet lit
four lanterns we hovered over like moths.

Now, only my phosphorescent toes
in two tight circles of electric blue.
Now, only a parlor trick of cells,
of dinoflagellates disturbed
in their long swim somewhere else.

Days That Should Have Been Yours

Damp earth and honeysuckle rise into the air
I am left with. The roses rise, too. Roots stretch and push
through last year's leaves. It is almost too much

to be asked to breathe this—to take into my lungs
what we waited for, to take in more than my share.
Here. I have something that belongs to you—

you, who used to say I was selfish. Don't you see
how I have changed? There is too much sunlight,
too much blue and birdcall for me to keep alone.

My lips are always moving now, the way the lips
of a madwoman move. I know there is no one
to hear me. This is what shows I am sane.

Each evening the purple comes down so that I
might walk through it without being seen.
No one knows me here. No one can see my face.

Night keeps confessions—a priest asleep
on the other side of the screen—but tomorrow
the light will crack through—will force me

to step into it, to live in its glare. To know again:
you are not. To bear witness each morning to the waste
of more world than I can live in on my own.

Faith

I would be done with you—a melodrama limping feebly
to its denouement, a torch song untangling its last note.

I would fold and bury you at the bottom of a drawer,
something embarrassing and overwrought written long ago.

I can hold you now to stark light and note exactly how shoddy
the craft, how rote the lines. But still, I cannot bring myself

to stop reciting you—each unbidden syllable a clumsy bird
rising from a pond, sky-mad even on its stunted wings.

Thanks for Asking

Oh, I'm fine, fine—fit as a fiddle strung tight,
fit as a stepsister in a glass shoe. The mind has been

a bag of cats carried across a creek of slick stones.
Yet I've managed; I still have every one of those

scrabblers, the graffiti of their little tempers up
and down my spine. I summered in the bee-loud glade

between my ears, buzz so raucous sometimes I couldn't
hear bones pop or scars click their tiny needles.

True, I am as pale as a larva. Sunlight was not a part
of my regimen. I breathed the dark earth and grew ready.

But I wasn't lazy—there was industry in all the clay
I hollowed, the pots I threw and left to harden into

vessels that could hold slough, poisons, loose change.
I concur—everyone needs a break, whether *from* or *in* or *down*—

I took mine breakneck, on the runaway horse of August;
I took mine on two wheels, pumping at empty floorboards.

Yes, glad to be back—back on track, back singing backup,
doo-wop to an old tune—back wielding my arsenal of pushpins,

folding flat words into origami, brandishing unsnapped chalk
to draw a map of where I've been and where I'm bound.

2 a.m.

In the spring of three-hour nights, she wakes with the white
lozenge of the moon stuck in her throat, dreams as sheer
as coconut shavings scattered over the pillow.

Lunacy prickles her skin like the onset of influenza until
even air is too heavy, a silk scarf of stickpins.
The sleepers in the house leak static through the walls.

It will be another morning as powdery as bone—the staccato
of a trapped moth in her wrist. All day she will navigate
through the ragged islands of eyes and voices,

her raft leaking dread through thin, lashed timbers.
Somewhere distant, dusk's purple creed is prayed;
sleep is a dot of landfall she can blot out with one thumb.

The Secret

All your life, you could never
keep a secret. How to hold tight
the gem that would be shiny only
if it could be lifted to the light?
How to keep one's word
heavy on the tongue instead of
launching it into the listening air?

In the dark between our twin beds
was the motherless, fatherless world
we had made. There we told each other
stories prefaced by oaths of silence.
Swear, because if you tell, then
God will strike you dead. And yet,
each time you told, somehow, you lived.

As the secrets grew bigger, I stopped
sharing them. The covert strategies,
the subterfuge I studied, you took
as a slap, a gauntlet thrown, and crafted
techniques to lay bare all that I worked
so hard to hide. You were the enemy,
the spy, the villain, who, against all odds,

I loved. What was between us always
was riddled with cracks, glued, re-
cracked, reassembled, each time with less
skill and greater need. What was never

a secret was that I knew I could not live
without you. But even that, dumb luck
has proven wrong. Now the only secret

you have ever kept is between us.
Like a locked door. Like a stone
not rolled away. I rise blind into
every morning, inch forward through
the unlit day. At last you have learned
silence—or have become it. From this
I must judge between the quiet and the gone.

The Idea of Heaven

I don't believe in it

except when alone, walking
straight into an orange sun
as it eases itself out of the sky
and down into the trees,

as it taints the clouds
with the coral of its passing.
If a gull should cross
that scene, its wings

closing and closing,
and if rays of that sun's falling
should stretch out to me
like hands extended, like

beckoning, then I will open
my hard heart a little and say
your name, as though, if you still
exist anywhere, it must be here

in this periwinkle tint of
cumulus, in this silhouette
of feather and bone soaring
across light. I call it gull

but it could be any winged thing.
It is not there as bird, after all,
but as emissary. Unfettered
from logic, I confer upon it

your soul—a rumpled, unopened thing
I had not thought fit to unfold,
much less release into the wild.
What I say to the sky might

be thought a prayer, yet I do not
talk to any god, but rather, to you.
No one overhears me unless
I am mistaken about all of it.

I lift up my myth on the chance
of being wrong, to this heaven
that looks like beauty,
burning. That looks like

the sort of heaven you
would have dreamed, the story
you would have told, if you
had been given the chance.

From the Back Seat

Before we had ever heard of mandatory restraints,
of Newton's Laws of Motion, my sister and I moved
through summers and over interstates, unbuckled,
loose as picked apples, in the back seat
of a 1955 sky blue Pontiac sedan.

Beyond the rush and buffet of air through always
open windows were cornfields broken by rest stops
and bird-spattered picnic tables, lanes of concrete
bordered by gullies glinting with green shards
of bottle glass. A hazy shimmer of heat made our skin

stick to the vinyl, our hair to our faces, as we dozed
over miles we did not have to count or navigate.
Murmur of front-seat voices lulled a way for letting go
of the getting-there, opened a hole through time
that made the arriving seem both mystical

and humdrum. If I could wish us anywhere now,
it would be to one of those earlier journeys, lying
head-by-feet across wherever we were going, driven by
hands we knew. Before we learned there were other
hands at the wheel. Perhaps no hands at all.

Trespassing

In this deceptive spring, the animals
seem bolder—as though somehow
they have gotten word
that it is their world now.

Our retreat into our houses,
our sequestered safe zones,
turns the yards and walkways into
wilderness more theirs than ours.

When I dare to venture out,
the squirrels do not scatter so much
as shun me for my audacity.
The crows caw indignation

from the trees and phone lines,
shocked that I should presume
to breathe their air, to peer
into their sky.

This evening when I open my door
I find a rabbit on the stoop
looking in at me. Will it bolt when I break
this boundary, when I infiltrate its dominion?

I hesitate—
and we look long at one another,
the quick breath in our bodies translating
what we don't know how to say.

When at last I step into
the changed world, the rabbit leaves
me to it, not fleeing so much as offering me
a small life I can still call mine.

Five

Waiting for You

I open my ears, my pores, press the tips of my fingers
into the farthest air. You promised you would return.
Whatever there is that could be closed in this house,

in me, is ajar. I invite you to sit down beside me,
wait for the sofa cushion to dip and steady, listen hard
into the noise that is the only white thing in this darkness

for you to speak my name or at least to whisper, sigh,
to let me know you are there. Here it is not only you
who has no body. Here we can be only the shapes we make

of our thoughts. All those terrible months after your death,
I threw words into space in case you were there to catch them,
but now what words I have left I merely set

beside me like lures. There is no light here to find them,
to turn them into glint and flash. But still, I am waiting.
If there should come at last a signal, I think it will not be mine.

You Knew a Woman

Because I am contained here, you will not
find me. Your eyes will see what holds me,
but not what is held. I may walk past you now

as an unglazed clay pot, a cardboard box
with movable legs that might astonish you
if you knew how they once danced,

a man's hands damp against the hollow
of my back, his touch the guide that helped me
find the rhythm. That beat is still in the floorboards,

but the feet learn restraint, shun the unseemly.
The shapes a squat container may contain
are superfluous, a cargo of stones, a hold

freighted with drag. I live alone here,
lonely in my bones. I do not sway, but plod.
And it is I—not you—who must measure time by this.

Low Tide

The sea breathes in and holds
the breath. Tidal pools brim
with what I have had to take
on faith: anemones, moon snails,
barnacles, cling fish. Seaweed
undulating like a beating heart.

Here, a harvest of cucumbers and stars.
Cones of limpets clasped to shells.
Clams cast up as gifts to gulls.
Even darkest secrets glitter in the sun—
a tentacled gorgon, the eel-flash
of a gunnel, stranded and dying.

Would that there were more
low tides: my narrow life, inhaled;
a curtain pulled back from a black window.
Ankle-deep, I would wade awake through angels
or sand. At sudden ebb, would dare my eyes
to look—into pools of zero—or of God.

Sudden Storm

Something pushes the thunderheads down, a thumb across
a throat. Leaves fly up and crows blow wrong as umbrellas.

A skittering over the roof tiles says *time to make tracks*.
Somewhere nearby, dead limbs are cracking their punch lines.

Those of us with bones unpitch our tents, the slick spikes loose
and dangerous in our hands. Now the decision to be made

is plain: run or succumb. And yet, we look back: the windows
down each tidy street steam with the pressed faces of the wives

of Lot. That crackle and snap is what we desire—to be in it
and still breathing. A zag of blue strikes the horizon and makes

its point. Something somewhere will burn and rise. The guzzling dirt
sends out refugees to take their chances in the changed air.

Vigilance

Because I watched,
because I posted sentries,
because I tied a bell to the knob before daring
sleep, left a jangle pending at every
window crank, a light burning across
pitch for rogues or radicals,
because this, because that, *because,*
all day all night, the hits just kept on coming,
my lungs opened, closed, like blooms in a hothouse,
my blood looped round and round on its toy track,
each morning turned on like a CD burned
years ago and left revolving in my car,
because and because
every sun sparked like ignition,
like recognition,
there was sorcery on my tongue
because
all night I fretted an abracadabra,
severed top from bottom, knotted
scarf to scarf, palmed coins,
tilted mirrors,
and ever ready
for razzle-dazzle,
lined
the rabbits,
the top hats,
in rows.

I Want to Say No

I want to say no, to resist, but one day follows another
like dingy geese into a pond—the paddle around
the leaf-clotted perimeter, obligatory and grim.

I wake each morning in the wrong body,
baffled, and dress, the knees, breasts, pores
of a mystery I wonder if anyone will solve

or want to. The eyes I paint aren't fooling
anyone. Sideways at the mirror, I peep
hard right to catch the woman others give

my name, try to smooth her like a rumpled
bed, but the knack is no longer mine.
And still I set this face toward the new day,

imagining that there might yet be someone
who will take my syllables between his lips
and tease from them a rhythm I can sway to,

refusing to give me back to the glass—who will
shake the maraca to buzz and loose
the seeds trapped inside impostor bones.

Dead Reckoning

Where you were, there is not even
an absence. The world is there instead,
filling up the space you claimed as yours.

It's physics, then. Remove the swimmer
from the water and the water rushes in
to fill the shape she made there.

In the weeks that followed your death,
your son, my daughter, your friends, even
people who barely knew you, confided to me

that you had appeared to them—hovering
at their shoulder, watching from a corner,
infiltrating their dreams. I have waited for

my turn, each night saying your name,
summoning you from the hissing darkness.
The air of my room moves only as the heat

pushes through the vents. On the other side
of the walls, my neighbor's pipes burble,
then still. Another friend claims that I write

about you now because you are pulling
strings from some other world, a puppeteer
from the afterlife with a desire to be known—

but my fingers on the keys are fingers
of wood. The hinge of my mouth creaks
and opens for sounds that no one puts on

my tongue. You made a vow to me
and I to you. Nothing would have kept you
from making good on your word

except that your words are gone. That you
are gone. There is no hole torn in the fabric
of the world. There is only the world.

The Last Living Speaker

—italicized lines from an article about Marie Wilcox

She is the last living speaker of Wukchumni,
a tribal tongue spoken in a valley called San Joaquin.

Every morning, while the coffee beside her sends up
its message of steam, Marie Wilcox hunts and pecks

at her keyboard to gather those dying words into a place
that will last, a dictionary that will survive her.

I understand that quest to archive what is kept in the self,
but lack her zeal. On evening walks I well with stories

that rise from what has been left to me.
My father, mother, sister, gone. Only I remain to tell

our lives as they really were, and even then,
I will tell them wrong—the facts straight, but not

the angle of light or the whisper of the hickory in early fall
or the tang of rain through the bedroom screen.

And worse, perhaps, no one will hear or care. I can't help
but mull on all the small worlds lost because there was nobody

who remained to recall. *No one seems to want to learn,*
Marie tells the one who asks. Her pages brim

with nouns and verbs, the sounds of her childhood,
uncertainly spelled, never known in any way

but aurally. Each night, pressing save to hold them
for anyone who thinks to follow her, she makes a mission

out of what she cannot let go. Impossible to look
dead-on at one's own extinction, to know that what burns

so blue and bright will gutter, go out without a hiss.
I dwell now inside an unpeopled place.

Those who walk with me are shadows on abandoned walls,
outlines in brass frames, names chiseled into stone.

No one would seek this burden. To be the hanger-on
who is left alone. Out of the past we linger in, we drag

whatever we can into open air. *It seems weird*, she says,
that I am the last one. She pushes the button on a tape recorder

and lets the revolutions reel in a myth she recites in the singsong
lilt of something learned by heart. What is now only an ache

inside me is not yet words; I cannot produce it by rote. How strange
that to be the last speaker left, one must also be the first.

Acknowledgments

The author gratefully acknowledges the editors of the following journals where these poems first appeared.

Anti-Heroin Chic: "The Body, Broken"

The Cincinnati Review: "If There Are Ghosts"

Diode Poetry Journal: "2 a.m.," "I Want to Say No," "Sudden Storm"

Fourteen Hills: "This Dog"

Rust + Moth: "Ocean"

Southern Poetry Review: "From the Back Seat," "The Sound of It"

Summerset Review: "Incursion"

Tar River Poetry: "Tell the Birds," "What Burned in the Sky"

The Threepenny Review: "If Time Travel Is Possible"

Valparaiso Poetry Review: "Language Lessons," "The Night Divers"

UCity Review: "Capitulations," "The Idea of Heaven," "You Knew a Woman"

"Endangered" was featured on *Autumn Sky Poetry Daily* on May 2, 2022.

About the Author

Melanie McCabe's poetry collection, *What The Neighbors Know*, was published by FutureCycle Press in 2014, and was awarded an Honorable Mention in the Library of Virginia's Literary Awards competition. Her first collection, *History of the Body*, was published by David Robert Books in 2012. Her nonfiction book, *His Other Life: Searching for My Father, His First Wife, and Tennessee Williams*, won the University of New Orleans Press Lab Prize, and a feature article about it appeared in *The Washington Post* in December of 2017. Her poems have appeared in *The Georgia Review*, *The Threepenny Review*, *Alaska Quarterly Review*, *The Massachusetts Review*, *The Cincinnati Review*, and elsewhere. Her work has also appeared on *Poetry Daily*, *Verse Daily*, and in *Best New Poets 2010*. She lives in Falls Church, Virginia, and taught high school English for twenty-two years.